Pebble® Plus

Creepy Crawlers

Camel Spiders

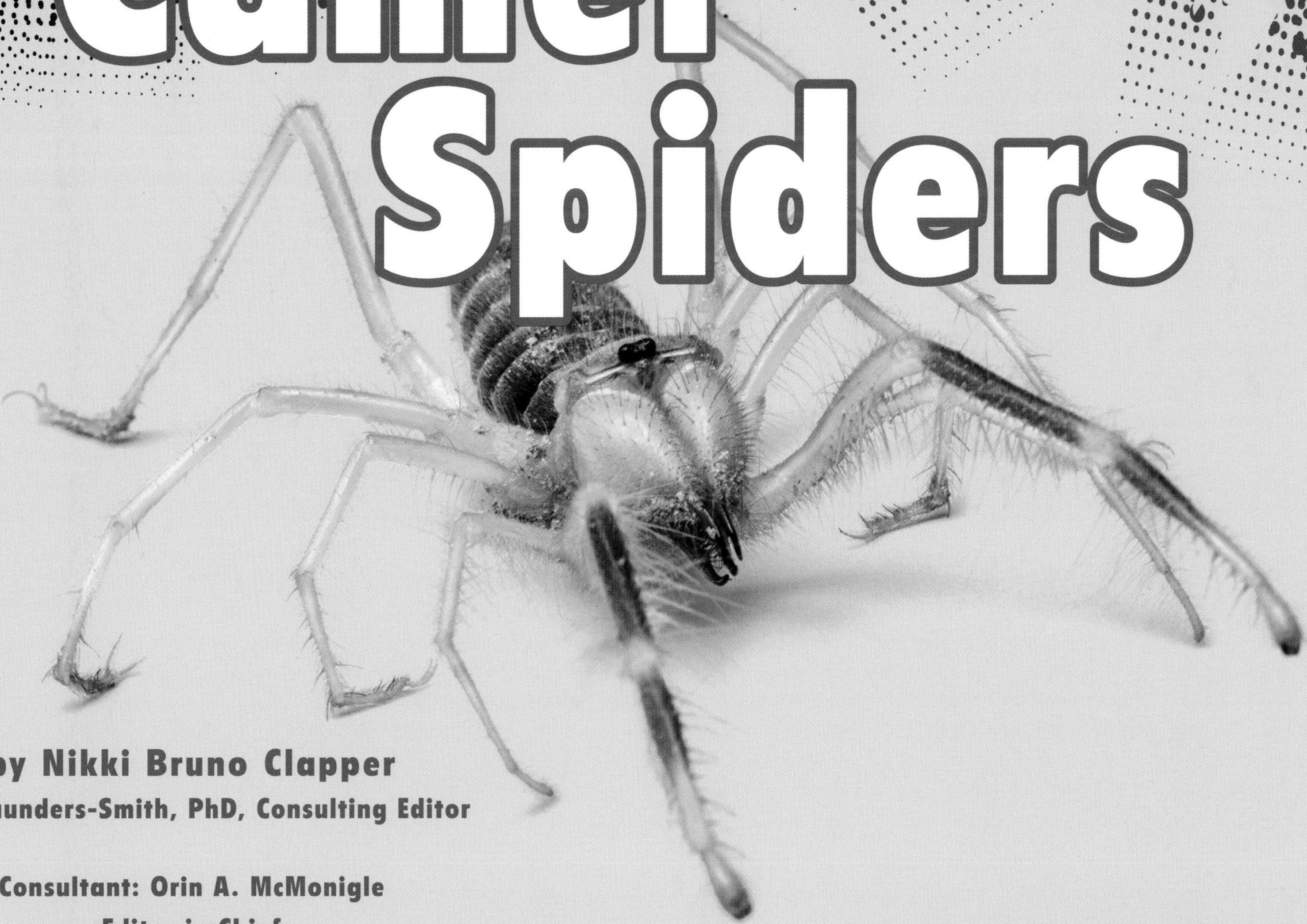

by Nikki Bruno Clapper

Gail Saunders-Smith, PhD, Consulting Editor

Consultant: Orin A. McMonigle
Editor in Chief
Invertebrates Magazine

CAPSTONE PRESS
a capstone imprint

Pebble Plus is published by Capstone Press,
1710 Roe Crest Drive, North Mankato, Minnesota 56003.
www.capstonepub.com

Library of Congress Cataloging-in-Publication Data
Clapper, Nikki Bruno, author.
Camel spiders/by Nikki Bruno Clapper.
pages cm.—(Pebble Plus. Creepy Crawlers)
Summary: "Simple text and full-color photographs introduce
camel spiders"—Provided by publisher.
Audience: Ages 4–8.
Audience: K to grade 3.
Includes bibliographical references and index.
ISBN 978-1-4914-6216-4 (library binding)
ISBN 978-1-4914-6228-7 (ebook pdf)
1. Solpugida—Juvenile literature. 2. Spiders—Juvenile literature.
I. Title. II. Series: Pebble Plus. Creepy Crawlers.
QL458.8.C53 2016
595.4'8—dc23   2015008491

Editorial Credits
Michelle Bisson and Jeni Wittrock, editors; Juliette Peters, designer; Katy LaVigne, production specialist

Photo Credits
Alamy: INTERFOTO, 13; Getty Images: De Agostini Picture Library, 11; James P. Rowan, 7; Minden Pictures:
Piotr Naskrecki, 5; Newscom: Minden Pictures/Mark Moffett, 15, 17, 21; Science Source: Francesco Tomasinelli, 9;
Shutterstock: Ivan Kuzman, 19, wacpan, cover, 1

Design Element
Shutterstock: vlastas66

Note to Parents and Teachers

The Creepy Crawlers set supports national science standards related to biology and life
science. This book describes and illustrates camel spiders. The images support early readers
in understanding the text. The repetition of words and phrases helps early readers learn new
words. This book also introduces early readers to subject-specific vocabulary words, which are
defined in the Glossary section. Early readers may need assistance to read some words and
to use the Table of Contents, Glossary, Read More, Internet Sites, Critical Thinking Using the
Common Core, and Index sections of the book.

Printed in the United States of America in North Mankato, Minnesota.
052015   008823CGF15

Table of Contents

Jaws of Doom

A hairy, spiderlike creature
grabs an insect in an instant.
Then it uses sharp, strong
jaws to crush the prey.
It is a camel spider attack!

5

What Is This Creature?

People call this creature
a camel spider or a
wind scorpion. But it is
not a spider or a scorpion.
It is called a solifuge.

say it like this
SOL-i-fyooj

7

Solifuges can be very big. Some types are 6 inches (15 centimeters) long from leg to leg. They have two eyes behind their jaws.

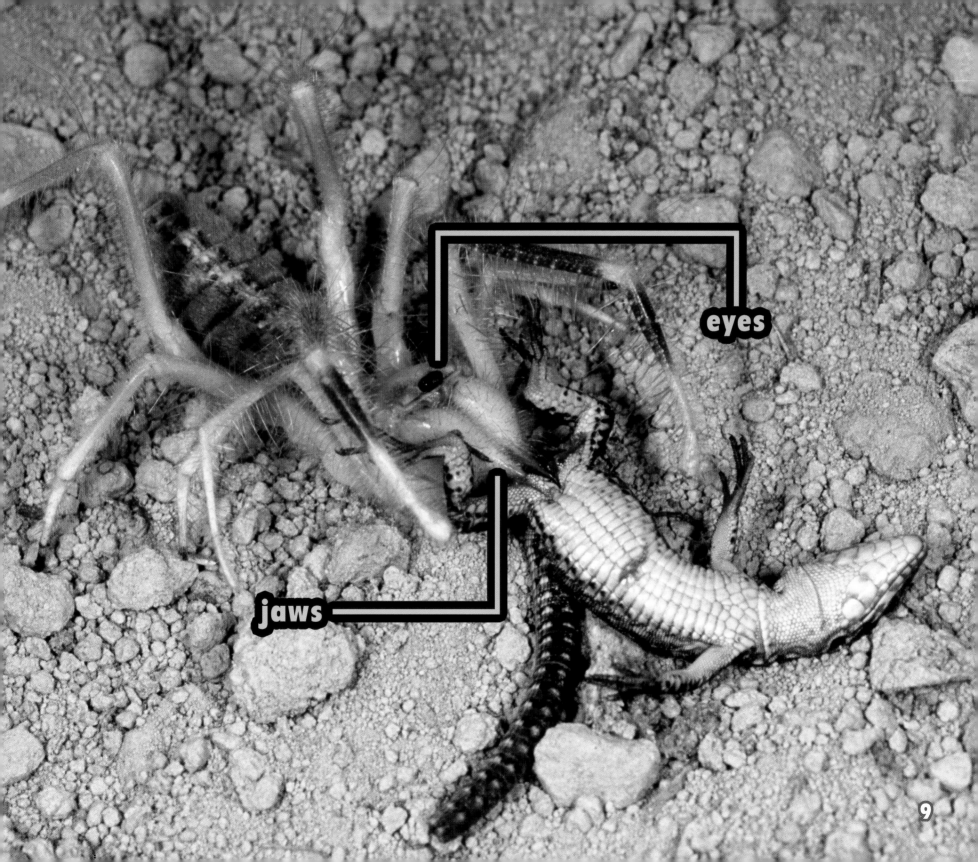

eyes

jaws

Camel spiders look like they have 10 legs. But the front two "legs" are pedipalps. These organs help solifuges feel what is around them.

pedipalps

Rulers of the Desert

Camel spiders live in hot deserts on most continents. They dig burrows in sand, soil, or pebbles. Burrows help them stay out of the hot sun.

Speedy Predators

Camel spiders can run up to 10 miles (16 kilometers) per hour. They chase prey such as insects, small lizards, and scorpions. Watch out!

camel spider
eating a scorpion

Solifuges catch prey with the sticky tips of their pedipalps. They grind their jaws back and forth to chew their prey.

Many people are afraid of camel spiders. But solifuges are not a danger to humans. Their bites are painful but have no venom.

A Year of Life

Female solifuges lay 20 to 200 eggs in a burrow. Baby camel spiders hatch from the eggs after about four weeks. They live for about one year.

Glossary

burrow—a tunnel or hole in the ground made or used by an animal

desert—a dry area with little rain

continent—one of Earth's seven large land masses

organ—a body part that does a certain job

pedipalp—a leglike limb that helps solifuges feel their surroundings and catch prey

predator—an animal that hunts other animals for food

prey—an animal hunted by another animal for food

scorpion—an arachnid with large pincers and a jointed tail tipped with a venomous stinger

solifuge—a member of a group of arachnids called camel spiders or wind scorpions

venom—a poisonous liquid produced by some animals

Read More

Anderson, Sheila. *What Can Live in a Desert?* Animal Adaptations. Minneapolis: Lerner Publications, 2011.

Murphy, Julie. *Arachnids.* Weird, Wild, and Wonderful. New York: Gareth Stevens Pub., 2010.

Murphy, Julie. *Desert Animal Adaptations.* Amazing Animal Adaptations. Mankato, Minn.: Capstone Press, 2012.

Internet Sites

FactHound offers a safe, fun way to find Internet sites related to this book. All of the sites on FactHound have been researched by our staff.

Here's all you do:

Visit *www.facthound.com*

Type in this code: 9781491462164

Super-cool stuff!

Check out projects, games and lots more at
www.capstonekids.com

Critical Thinking
Using the Common Core

1. What body parts do camel spiders use to catch prey? (Key Ideas and Details)

2. If camel spiders are not a danger to humans, why do you think many people are afraid of them? (Integration of Knowledge and Ideas)

Index

Word Count: 220
Grade: 1
Early-Intervention Level: 20